The Way We Be

The Way We Be

POETRY, PROSE, AND PROSETRY

Loretta (Firekeeper) Hawkins

All rights reserved. No part of this publication may be reproduced or transmitted in any form or by any means, electronic or mechanical, including photocopy, recording, or any information storage and retrieval system, without permission in writing from the publisher.

Requests for permission to make copies of any part of this work should be emailed to:
firekeeperartistry@gmail.com

Copyright © 2017 Loretta A. Hawkins

All rights reserved.

ISBN: 10: 0692957413
ISBN-13: 978-0692957417

PUBLISHED BY:
FIREKEEPER ARTISTRY
CHICAGO, ILLINOIS

DEDICATION

The Way We Be is dedicated to the young poets, artists, performers and the youth of today, for they have inspired me. When I elected to become a spoken-word artist about a year and a half ago, I did not imagine then that I would ever meet so many poets and so many young people. Their intelligence, energy, cleverness, commitment, and sheer kindness have all but overwhelmed me.

Although I had been writing poetry since I was thirteen, and then wrote extensively during later years, it was always a lonely and quiet love. Joining the spoken-word community has taken poetry to a higher level and created for me, a whole new world. The young poets accepted me so lovingly and respectfully that one can only say, they honored me. I struggle to keep up with them in so many ways, and their profound perspectives on the world order have challenged me to write better, do better, and be better. My quest is to be as brave as their brave young souls.

POETRY

We Be	1
Oh, Say Can You See	2
Like A Burning Sun	4
"All White People Are Not Against Us, "She Said"	5
Five Families	8
Willie Stole a Candy Bar	11
Slavery Deniers	14
I Was There	17
Free Stuff	20
The Ballad of Trayvon Martin	22
A Sonnet For My Mother	27
Human Shoes	28
Klan Lai	30
Snakes in Da Back	31
Alligator Bait	33
Only One Thing	35
We Who Are Black	37

Poetry Content cont...

Procreate	40
1993	43
God Sends An Angel	47
Slavery Ways	49
God Writes for Me	51
Enough	52
Black Like Me-It's A Rap	54
The Way We Be	59

Prosetry and Prose

Watermelon	62
Still	65
The Greyhound Bus Trip	68
Kenyans' Intellect	73
The Train Ride	74

PREFACE

Most of the poems in this book are not beautiful. They are not even pretty. What prevents them from being either, other than my writing skills, is their dominating theme of injustice. Injustice is not, and by its nature cannot be, beautiful. The purpose of writing these poems was not a quest for beauty, but rather a need to expose truth. Truth can be evasive, hidden or forgotten. It can be vague and even forbidden. In the absence of truth, hypocrisy triumphs.

The truth is, America has long proclaimed itself to be the land of the brave and the home of the free. This misnomer existed, even though three centuries of practicing human slavery. Hypocritically, to protect and justify this illusion of freedom, humans who were slaves in this country, were declared, by law, to be *not completely human*, but three-fifths, human. Otherwise, how does one proclaim itself to be the land of liberty while enslaving a tenth of its *human* population?

The institution of slavery was characterized by inhumanity, brutality, and savagery on the part of the slave owners, in particular, and a majority of Southern white citizens in general. Slaves were whipped, mutilated, raped and or executed daily, and prohibited, by law from learning to read or write. Overworked, underfed, devoid of medical care and daily brutalization resulted in premature deaths of large numbers of slaves.

After centuries of slavery, and with the signing of the Emancipation Proclamation, the United States had an opportunity to redeem itself, a chance to apologize and seek redemption. It did neither. Conversely, it did the exact opposite! The United States government allowed the previous slave states to impose and enact vicious law systems, that applied only to black Americans, that prevented ex-slaves, freedmen and mulattoes from advancing economically, socially, and educationally. These laws, called the Black Codes, virtually plunged African-Americans back into slavery, but now without providing the slave the meager protection that their previous slave-owners had afforded them.

The Black Codes provided the answer to what white Americans would do without the free black labor that slavery had afforded them. The Black Codes Vagrancy Laws, instituted first by the state of Mississippi, and quickly and enthusiastically followed by all previously slave states, western states, and even northern states, put into motion the dynamics that would impact race relations in America to the present day.

The impact and influence of post-slavery actions adversely affecting African-Americans are well documented. White Supremacists, Neo-Nazi, , and Alt-Right advocates would do well to read some of these works. If, after reading *Slavery By Another Name* by Douglas Blackmon, *American Apartheid, Segregation and the Making of the Underclass* by Nancy Denton and Massey; *The Condemnation of Blackness :Race, Crime, and the Making of Modern Urban America,* by Khilil Gibran Muhammad and *The New Jim Crow: Mass Incarceration in the Age of Colorblindness* by Michelle Alexander, those groups continue to hate; one can only conclude that those hate-mongers possess not only sincere ignorance, but also sincere hatred. What is notable about the above works is that their primary focus is not slavery, but the egregious treatment of blacks after slavery ended.

The poems, prosetry and prose in this book are my ancestral catharsis.

ACKNOWLEDGMENTS

Thanking my mother, Laurine Hines Sanders, for reciting poetry to me when I was a child, and instilling in me my great love of poetry. Thank you, Mom!!

I wish to thank my book formatter, Jasmine Cummings for making it happen with this project. Through it, all she kept her head up, working long hours into the night to meet deadlines and ensuring that the project moved smoothly along. Thanking her for the beautiful book covers that she created for this and my other books. Thanking her for tolerating my episodes of panic, which threw her into peals of laughter. Her laughter calmed my fears. Thank you, Jasmine Cummings!

"They tried to bury us, but they did not know that we were seeds."

POETRY

WE BE

I be
you be
he, she, it be

we be
you be
they be.

How simple.
How un- der- stand- able
But teacher say:
I can't be
I have to am
you have to are
and he is – and she.
we, like you, have to are

and they, of course
being plural are too.
but teacher don't
un – der- stand that
all the time
all the time

me, my mama, pa
all of us
us,
we be.

OH, SAY CAN YOU SEE?

oh, say can you see, can you see the africans running, running away from the men without skin, running from the loud, over-powering sticks that kill, running from their chains and whips, trying to stand as free men in the battle's confusion, running from their unknown future, running, can you see them

oh, say can you see, can you see the africans on ships, the middle passage, running to the ship's edge, trying to leap into an ocean where there is no land in sight, determined to swim back to land – or die trying, running into the mists of the deep, running to the gloom of their underwater graves, running and leaping, can you see them

oh say can you see, can you see slaves in america, running away from the horrors and insanity of slavery, trying to run but not knowing where there is land that is free, running, knowing that if caught, no refuge could save them, following the north star, running under moonlight and bright stars trying to escape from this land of the free, running north, still running at dawn's early light, running to an unknown future, putting god in their trust, running, can you see them

oh, say can you see, can you see african americans in america's south, after slavery ended, running, running from the , the lynchings, the burnings at the stakes, the home and church bombings bursting in air that gave proof through the nights and days, that the flag and equality were merely an illusion, they were not there, running from hound-dogs and jails, running in fear, running in the last gleam of twilight from sadistic savages masquerading as humans, running, can you see them

oh say can you see, can you see black people today, running, running for our lives, running from police whose mission, it seems, is to kill us, as we try to run away, running to stay alive from police who kill unarmed citizens with impunity, under the banner that is spangled with stars, running to stay alive, running in perilous flight, running, running, can you see us, can you see us, oh, say can you see, oh, say can you see, can you see?

LIKE A BURNING SUN

Injustice against one, which is sanctioned by a
government of which one is a citizen
Is like a burning sun.
The sun is Earth's life source – without which we
would all perish.
But what if the sun warped – became twice as hot
Than it is or should be? It would burn us if we ventured
out beneath it.
What would we Earthlings do?
If we found a way to survive, could we be happy?
Most likely not, for life would become
A constant struggle to survive.
That is what racial injustice is like – a burning sun.
It affects every aspect of our lives:
How we are born, how we live, how we die.
The heat consumes us.
Injustice, like a corrupted sun
Has no tolerance for human imperfections.
We die for failing to signal a lane change,
For missing a front license plate,
For jaywalking or selling loose cigarettes.
If a child, for playing with a toy gun in the park.
There are no apologies from the sun for killing us.
It is hot and deadly.
The sun burns us with impunity, without sympathy.
Many of us exist in a state of hopelessness
Knowing one cannot outrun a burning sun.

"ALL WHITE PEOPLE ARE NOT AGAINST US," SHE SAID
THE KILLING OF SANDRA BLAND

Sandra Bland is dead, and it can honestly be said, that she did not need to die. What events can there be, that allowed her to hang, not from a tree – like traditional lynching - but from a plastic bag? Although this tale is ludicrous and sad, it is also beyond belief. And as our black nation once again recoil in human grief, where there seems to be, no relief, we know deep inside, something has to be done if we, as a people, are to survive this burning sun.

Sandra Bland said, "All white people are not against us." And it is equally sad, that she didn't encounter the ones she could trust. But instead, she met a man. "You didn't signal a lane change," he said. Three days later, in a jail cell, she was dead.

Only one of two things could be written on the record that sat on the shelf: She was either murdered or she killed herself. Guess what it said? It's ludicrous and sad. She hanged herself with a plastic bag! So we go back and look at the cam video and the events that took place, let us know, that Sandra would not get out of this alive – and the events would not be dignified. We who are black could so clearly see what the outcome of this tragedy was going to be. And in spite of the words of reconciliation that Sandra said – The problem revolved around the fact that she was *not* afraid.

Long ago, Willie Lynch wrote: to make a black person a nigger, without even having to pull a trigger – just keep the fear of God in them, and make sure they always respect and love white skin. But Sandra, we saw, had no such fear and she apparently did not sense that danger was near. The policeman we imagine, could see that too, and he was not quite sure what to do. "Is it possible," we think, to himself he said, "that this black woman before me is not afraid? Can't she see this uniform and white skin I wear? I'll light her up, on the confederate flag, I swear!"

Finally he found something to say, "You seem to be irritated." She responded she was because she was just trying to get out his way. Now here, this tale would be over – be ended – if he had said, "Here's your ticket – go on your way. But he couldn't or wouldn't let her go, because she was still unafraid, you know. Because she still had no fear, you know, he wouldn't - he wouldn't let her go! He asked her to put out her cigarette. Sandra spoke up promptly with no regrets. She defended her right to smoke in her own car. So he asked her to step out of her own car. We viewers could see on the video, this had gone way too far – but the crucial words came suddenly – You're under arrest! "For what? We ask. We'll just have to guess.

Outside of the car, they walk out of the cam's view. No one can now see what each will do. We only know she began to scream. Screaming in the now-hidden scene. I could go on and on and on, but why? We all know Sandra Bland did not have to die. The last time we saw her alive she was vibrant, defiant, refusing to be treated unjustly, and remain compliant. Yet, they'll have us believe she went from that state of pride, to one of utter despair and suicide. We, the black nation believe none of this – as we grit our teeth, hold up a Ballad fist – contemplating this tragic twist.

We've heard before this sad, sad song, as we wait for the grand jury to declare police did no wrong. This country continues, for us, to be a killing land, where black people have never had ground on which to stand. Black people in America live in a police state, where police, with us, constantly instigate. They throw us to the ground, on our backs put their knee, they chock us, they shoot us as we try to run, you see. They even still now, hang us from a tree - In this land of the brave, in this home of the free.

They still burn our churches, thinking we will no longer pray. They mass-incarcerate us by the hundreds every day. The mayors of cities spend tax dollars in neighborhoods that are white, pretending that they think that that is alright. In black neighborhoods, they close the school's doors. An action that will keep us poverty-stricken and poor. There are many ways to treat a people unfairly, without ever, hanging them from a tree, or holding them down with your evil knee. Yes, this country is still, for us, a killing land, and the last one it killed was Sandra Bland.

FIVE FAMILIES

Trayvon Martin, Michael Brown and Tamir Rice
Were all shot and killed, then *they* were accused of committing vice.
While Eric Gardner was simply choked 'til he had no breath
And could only lie on a New York Street, and succumb to death.
John Crawford stood in Walmart, holding an unwrapped toy gun.
Two cops appeared – John Crawford – couldn't even run !
Five black males, without guns, all lost their lives
While five white males – with guns- went home to wives.
Five families – whose lives were shot and completely shattered
Because five grand juries decided, "Black lives don't matter."
Five white grand juries, five white defending attorneys
Proved beyond doubt , that five black males deserved final journeys.
Felt white males, all pursuing, with a legal gun
Could stand their ground and had no *need* to run.
But five black males, without a gun, the juries found
Deserved to die – because they had no ground.
How can black people stand ground – when there is no ground?
Instead of ground, there's quicksand, we have found.
For instance, Marissa Alexander, a young, educated wife
In fear of an abusive husband and fearing for her life

Shot a warning bullet into a solid wall
Which began her plunge into an epic fall.
Although police reports supported the validity of her fears,
A grand jury sentenced Marissa to twenty years!
Twenty years – no one shot, no one dead
But she was imprisoned for being black and afraid.
When will this insanity on African- Americans stop?
We feel like we living on a dynamite spinning top!
When will the United Nations take a stand?
And declare a moratorium - declare a ban
On killing black people in America because we're black.
America! We charge you with genocide!
An historical record from which you *cannot* hide.
These killing are modernized lynchings of today
For evil is real – and it has found its way!
What is it that makes them want all of us dead?
What is it that makes them so intensely afraid?
Is it the melanin we possess that protects us from the sun?
That natural object from which some races must run?
Or is it the thing that makes an NBA coach who
Truly wants to win
Put on the floor, not four, but five black men?
Is it this thing of our natural physicality?
Bred into our genes from days of slavery?
Where those who survived the Middle Passage on the sea
Were then, force- bred with Mendes and Mandingos
So there would be *more* slaves,
To equal or surpass in numbers
Those dropped into underwater graves!

Dear God, we ask, where is their sanity?
That would lend to them some essence of humanity?
What is this thing that releases their savagery
And makes them think what's funny to see
Is other humans hanging from a tree
America! We charge you with genocide!
One day you'll try to explain how *hard* you tried.
And we will simply say, "But you always lied!"
A grand jury is nothing but a big, white boldface lie
That prevents innocent, American black youth from
 Living before they die.
But then one day there'll be nothing else to say.
For history has proven that evil cannot persist
For humans of good will always insist
That evil is relegated to a different space
Because racism has no relevancy in the human race,
Just as a beautiful flower has no value over another
And is never judged, by nature, based only on its color.
So too, with humans it is positively true
Your true value lies in that which God has bestowed
upon you.
So act -to change the laws, to protect innocent others
Realizing that all humans, under God, are human
brothers
And if you believe - in the Fatherhood of God
Must not you also believe in the brotherhood of man?
And an earth where five black families can live and
breathe in a more just land!

WILLIE STOLE A CANDY BAR

Willie stole a candy bar for the very last time.
Policemen shot the thief fourteen times!
Now it just so happens
Willie was today twenty-seven.
Folks exclaimed, "Good Lord! in heaven!
He was shot for almost every other year he was alive"
Folks all said, "What kind of jive is this?
And why is a grown man stealing a candy bar?
Now stealing a candy bar is not a serious kind of thing.
But dying face down on the streets has a serious ring.
But before I digress and go too far
Let's go back and explore this candy bar- stealing thing.
So why *would* a grown man steal a candy bar?
What kind of degradation has his life seen so far?
It's not like he committed murder, robbery or rape.
It's the equivalent of someone dying for the stealing of
a grape. It's like Jean Valjean in Les Miserables
Sentenced to twenty years in old Paris
For stealing a loaf of bread - O Mercy Me!
But that was before
France had its cultural revolution
Seeking to create a social solution
To injustice in France! They had a chance!
Cause the king fell down - and the people rose up!
And society in France became less corrupt!
Remember, the Louvre in Paris was the home of the
king,

While the masses of people didn't have anything!
But America doesn't even say, "Let them eat cake."
Declaring war on citizens is what America takes.
America just brings in its military drill-
The tanks, bayonets, and other things that kill
By their actions they declared war on Americans who are Black.
Said we'll kill them in a second
And historically, that is fact.
If he was running away - say you feared for your life!
Then beside his dead body place a gun or a knife!
Then have no worries - you will go free
Because you're white in this land –
This land of the free!
Now Willie as a baby ate some paint with lead.
And before the age of twelve , had ten times bled
From bullet wounds - and deep knife stabbings
And once in a riot, he was out there grabbing!
Trying to get something - Anything to have!
He was shot in his arm that youthful time
And luckily he was able to pay for his crime
But this time Willie's luck just plain ran out
And while lay dying in the street
 His Mama could only shout, "My baby! My baby! My baby is dead!"
Understand that now - Willie is - officially unafraid!
That he won't get a job or he won't get ahead!
It's irrelevant his system was tainted with lead!
Won't have to worry now 'bout eating stale bread!
Or worry 'bout the roaches crawling round in his bed!
Won't have to stand again, in a welfare line!
Or worry about doing more penitentiary time!

He won't have to steal - just so he can eat!
Or worry 'bout the raggedy shoes on his feet!
Not worry how the plumber's union wouldn't give him a card!
Or worry anymore because life's so hard!
Or worry how he couldn't support the kids and wife!
Before he lost them! Don't *even* worry about strife!
Like the years he couldn't get a job and lost all hope!
And how is desperation he had turned to dope!
He won't worry 'bout the drugs that have fried his brain!
Won't worry any more that he's no longer sane!
No, Willie now is free and he has gone far!
Because today Willie stole a candy bar!
Stole a "thing" in this land of the brave and the free!
Yes, today Willie found true liberty!
Succumbing to death, he had a moment to reflect
And because he understood cause and effect,
He was glad he hadn't put the candy back on the shelf.
He was glad that he was finally going to die
Because that meant that he would no longer have to try
To be a man in this land- this land of the brave.
This land where his slave- fathers forcefully gave
 Gave their sweat, gave their blood and their whipped- back tears
And died penniless like him, for countless years
When he closed his eyes for the very last time
His last rational thought was everything is fine.
Closing his eyes, he was shocked - shocked,
that he could so vividly see,
That his body, soul, and spirit were finally free.

SLAVERY DENIERS

In Texas, a school boy came home with a book, and we thank God today his mother read it and took a good look, for this book had an incredulous tale that it told of how America obtained its precious black gold. This book told of how our people, you see, came across the Atlantic unchained and free. These historical revisionists - they have a plan, to show how our people actually got to this land.

To make for 400 years a people your slave, then deny that it happened is even more grave, more egregious, and ludicrous and all kinds of bad, which makes you a liar, and all kinds of sad. And it's bad enough being a regular old liar, but to stoop to the depths of a slavery denier? Dear God! Their ancestors made us a slave; now their descendants drag their minds from the graves, and continue their macabre quest to end up in hell, because of their inability the truth to tell.

Now the book did not implicitly say we were *not* slaves, but more importantly it was the impression it gave, which was African-Americans were workers when we came over here, with no whips, no chains, without any fear! Just like folks who are immigrating here today. We were just immigrants, the book tried to say. But I know, and you know, and the book publishers know too, that that affirmation is utterly untrue.

Like in Germany, there were Germans who said there was no holocaust. It was not true that eleven millions lives were lost to barbaric savagery, to men gone insane, because those Germans deniers did not want to take blame.

Here in America, slavery deniers made up this Lie to say, because of reparations, which they don't want to pay. But, if we allow this incredulous lie to stand, what accounts for why we are so far behind in this land? What accounts for why our people are so poor, why we are plagued with chronic crime at our door? Why we have such a preponderance of gangs and thugs? Why our people are plagued with dangerous illegal drugs? Why mayors trap us into inferior schools? Why for black people a different set of rules? We're not fools! We understand you are rich because you made us poor. And our requests for reparations, you now ignore.

In Germany, the Lie made the Jewish people so upset, they raised holy hell, until Germany made it against the law a Denier Lie to tell. Yes, in Germany today, you will definitely go to jail, if a Denier Lie you dare to tell.

But your consciousness, in America, is bothering you, you see, so you try to pretend black people were always free. Again if we allowed this Lie to stand, next you'll be saying we actually sneaked into this land! Yes, we sneaked here with the few black immigrants that came. Yes, we sneaked here, that will be your next lying game! We even have proof that black people snuck in, we have pictures of them hiding in the dark spaces within, American ships transporting sugar, and gin. "You sneaked in," you'll say, "in the hull of our ships, in the dark, like sardines, hiding, lying flat on your back. And because you all sneaked here all sneaky like that, America has a right to ship all of you back." Incredulous thoughts, you dare to say? Not as incredulous as the Lie you told today. A Lie you deliberately wrote and put in a textbook, until a black mother took a thorough look.

As long as your people held us in abject slavery, at least, at least, let the truth travel free. Understand this, we will not allow you to rewrite our history, as long as one of us has breath that breathes, and an eye that can see.

I WAS THERE

I saw you when you came out of your mother's womb.
I saw you before you took your first breath of air – I
was there.
I heard you utter your first passionate cry. My joy at
that moment mixed with profound relief my daughter
and you didn't die.
I try to remember how small and vulnerable you were.
Seeing you now, so tall and fine, I wonder why I'd had
such a scare.
For birth is such a naturally beautiful kind of thing –
amazing all at the joy it brings.
I said a silent prayer at the hour of your birth, that
you'd survive – not just this hour – but from the perils
of the earth!
I was old enough to realize that there were evil spirits
out there. Waiting for you, hoping you would come.
The evil forces did not know how we would nourish
you – cherish you, make you intelligent and strong.
How we prayed to God that out there nothing would go
wrong.
And now, as your mother sits close to you, as she cries,
and sighs and pines – I remember Einstein said: great
spirits have always encountered violent opposition from
mediocre minds.
I saw you when you had your first real date – how
nervous you were as you sat to wait for her to come.
To some – you appeared to be a nervous mess.

You were wearing that black blazer that you liked best – but I knew all would go well - for who could possibly know – but not love you.

I saw you when you graduated university that last time. I was there. Swollen with pride to see you achieve your goals. I saw you on the stage look out and I saw you seeing me, seeing you. I felt so free!

Thinking you, you are the hope and the dream of the slave. The slave the slave-catchers hanged from a tree, because he broke the law and tried to be free. Now there you stood with a Ph.D.

You are a direct descendant of that courageous slave, and I was glad that we gave you all you needed to manifest your destiny.

I saw you when you kissed your beautiful bride. I was there. Lighting a candle with *her* grandmother, the flames uniting to join our families – back through the centuries and going forward – into eternity!

I heard you when you called me to say, that that day, you had just become a new dad. I was glad! You were on your way!

I remember later turning on the TV. My brain seemed dead, but my eyes could see. The caption read: unarmed black male dead! It was you! What could have happened? What did you do?

We later learned you were driving to the hospital, the light changed red, but you ran through. Police pulled you over – they shot you! Seventeen times.

Shot number nine was in the head. You were instantly dead. The police, of course said, he was afraid. The grand jury concurred that that verdict was fine.

Barack Obama at inauguration said, "Change will not come if we wait for some other person or some other time. We are the ones we have been waiting for." We are here!!!

FREE STUFF

Some white people love to talk about the free stuff black people get. And when I hear that nonsense, I invariably get upset. The reason I get upset is because in the alternative world where white people dwell, historical facts and reality tell a different tale. White people are the ones who have gotten the most stuff free! First, they stole this land from the Native Americans and killed them with impunity! So the first free stuff somebody got: this land was free!
Then they stole our bodies from Africa and brought them across the sea. The bodies that did not live because of the cruelty whites gave, were thrown into the ocean, into cold, underwater graves. And they have the gall, the nerve, the complete audacity - to open their mouths and talk about black people getting something free!
Once here in America, they proceeded to make us their slaves. So free labor is the free stuff black people gave. Free labor that made them and this country - beyond extremely wealthy. So our black labor - to them was free!
They came down to slave quarters, in the darkness of the night and raped our black women as though it were their right. Free sex they got for centuries, creating a new black American breed. And you have to admit free sex is something free. It became the essence of the white man's creed. So that's what they got free!

They stole our freedom – they stole our liberty! Our right to walk this earth as free beings. They stole our mobility! A thing that for them was free. But not for me. So that was free! For centuries they would not let us vote in this so –called democracy. But they voted, to determine who would rule. Their right to vote was free. So, votes for them were free!

Southern plantations and mansions were built by slaves, so they should belong to me. The White House in Washington – built by slaves – that was free! The highways, why don't they belong to me? The railroads in America. They got those railroads free! I could go on and on and on telling of thing that they got free. So tell me please why they still have them? Why don't they belong to me? And by me I mean black people, who toiled for years and years, through sweat and blood, in broiling sun, through whipped-back tears! So when white people talk about free stuff, you do realize, I trust - that the greatest free stuff white people got - their free stuff was us!

THE BALLAD OF TRAYVON MARTIN

He was a beautiful, beautiful boy, you know, a beautiful, beautiful boy.
With eyes that were bright and wondrous, that reflected his inner joy.

He was riding the cusp of manhood, he was carrying some Skittles and tea
He was talking to Rachel on his cell phone, asking what could
 the score possibly be.

He was laughing and talking to his good friend, who was home in the town of Miami.
When suddenly he became serious and said to her, "A man is following me."

We do not know exactly what happened that night - don't know who played what part.
We only know that a few moments later, the boy had a hole through his heart.

He was a beautiful, beautiful boy, you know, a beautiful, beautiful boy.

The neighbors could hear him screaming, he was pleading for a chance to live

But his killer, who stalked him lawfully, had no more chances to give.

For after all, the killer said, the boy was suspicious, was black
So he called 911 – got out of his car – followed the boy and at….

And yes! It was the boy who was screaming - I affirm this to all the land.
For how could the killer scream at all, if his mouth was covered by the boy's hand.

And if the boy was not covering his mouth, and the killer was able to shout.
Then he was not suffocating, as he claimed, for the two rule each other out.

So any way you take it, any way you say, the killer was telling a lie
And a jury believed his pack of lies – said it was right that the boy did die.

Now, come on people – Come on y'all, what kind of something is that?
That the victim caused him own death because, well, I guess because he was black!

He was a beautiful, beautiful boy you know, a beautiful, beautiful boy

He had no business being black – in that neighborhood, that is
So the neighborhood watchman followed him, carrying a gun and no fears.

Right off the screen of Cornbread, Earl and Me – where the innocent Cornbread was shot.
But the difference here, which of course, you know, this killer wasn't even a cop.

This killer, instead was a wanna-be cop – a man with a violent past
A man who called police 46 times, in the 24 months that just passed.

He was known for his vigilance of black boys, he was known to carry a gun
He was known to patrol Sanford streets at night – and at the rising of the sun.

The boy was innocent – without a clue. A manchild in a promised land.
Whose only crime was existing black, in a land we don't understand.

He was a beautiful, beautiful boy, you know. A beautiful, beautiful boy.

In this land of the free and this home of the brave, one truth I can surely surmise;

That the boy was not free – and his killer not brave
- but a beast that just men despise.

Yet the killer walks free, still spewing his lies –
while the boy lies beneath the ground.
And the rage that we feel, some can't understand -
it's a rage that makes our hearts pound.

He was a beautiful, beautiful boy, you know. A beautiful, beautiful boy.

Some think we won't remember – another Emmitt Till.
But our memories won't forsake us, and our spirits never will.

For pulsing through our bloodlines are ancient, monster crimes- of lynching's and castrations
From antiquated slavery times!

He was a beautiful, beautiful boy, you know. A beautiful, beautiful boy.

With precious, precious dark skin tones- Like Lauren Hill's, "The Sweetest Thing."
With hue and cry – we all now shout, "Let Freedom ring!"

As Martin said: Let freedom ring! But NO! Let freedom scream!

Let freedom scream and justice fall, like slanting rain.

So beautiful boys may have a chance to live again! Where beautiful boys can metamorphose into beautiful men.

He was a beautiful, beautiful boy, you know. A beautiful, beautiful boy! Amen.

A SONNET FOR MY MOTHER: YOU ARE THE ONE

Mom, you are the one that saved me – that gave me - Life
You are the one that taught me – fought for me – through strife
You are the one that believed in me – relieved me - from pain
You are the one that allowed me – to remain - sane.
You are the one that let me – that *bet* me – that I'd succeed
You are the one that allowed me – to believe
You are the one that cried for me – would die for me – and not blink
You are the one that stood by me – held me up – so I would not sink.
You are the one that I will show – that I know – your heart
And because of your maternity – for eternity – *we cannot part*
You are the one for whom my love goes on – and on forever
And for whom love shall not die – cannot die – not ever
As long as God's meandering rivers, can always find the sea
The precious love I have for you – will always simply – be.

HUMAN SHOES

"Yes, I immensely enjoy my shoes made of human leather!
I wear them every opportunity I have – I find the time.
Although I avoid wearing them in inclement weather.
You ask if I have any reservations, or whether
I feel wearing them is a crime.
No, I immensely enjoy wearing my shoes made of human leather.
Why? I suppose because they make me feel light as a feather.
I become a bird – ready to chime.
Although I do avoid wearing them in inclement weather.
You ask why I feel light as a feather?
It's odd because, black skin is thick, like a quarter, white skin thin as a dime.
Yet, I enjoy wearing my shoes made of human leather.
The tanning made them strong, rich black leather.
And no, they in no way feel like slime.
Maybe because I avoid wearing them in inclement weather.
No, I am unashamed wearing shoes made of black Negro leather
Yes, I understand they were someone's skin at some point in time.

But I do immensely enjoy my shoes made of human leather.
And to honor him, I avoid wearing them in inclement weather. "

Klan Lai

Ma ! They done caught Pa !
Dragged him with that ca'.
He dead.

Can't fight Klan or ba'
We must all run fa',
Instead.

What can we do, Ma?
We can't run too fa'!
We dead !!

Snakes in De Back

Driving, driving, Boston to Biloxi, beautiful country
Brand New car – 1937 Buick convertible
Visiting my sister - so many years have passed
Passing old plantations, majestic and grand, but guilty.
The weeping willows weep. Driving.
 Hot, dusty back road, running completely out of gas
Walking to nearby shack .
   Young woman in faded, ragged blue dress,
Cocoa skin, short –cropped black hair,
Sitting on porch, picking string beans.
"I'm willing to pay for help," I say.
 "You welcome to sit on de porch, in de shade, sir.
My brother, Willie, will go to Shell, sir, and git gas for you."
"Thank you."
 Bringing me cold lemonade, sitting with me, on steps
 Watching Willie ease down the dirt road, empty can in hand.
Old man in yard, walking back and forth, back and forth,
Speaking some strange kind of gibberish,
"*Pleasmastasirdon.*"
He has walked the grass away.
Is he speaking another language? I want to know.
"No sir," she says. " He got de snakes in deback."
Snakes in deback? What is that?
Calling old man to come. "Come," she gestures.
"Come up on de porch, Uncle Jake."
He comes up, without fear, mindless, eyes crazed.

"Pleamastasirdon," he tells the wind.
"Pleamastasirdon."
Is he speaking in tongues?
"No, sir. No sir. He just got de snakes in deback, that's all.

Dey make him crazy. Show him de snakes, Uncle Jake."

Pulling - a used-to-be- white shirt - up - then off.
Gibbering p*leamastasirdon.* In monotone, over and over.
Like words frozen and swollen in his cognition, erasing all others.
Woman saying, "Turn around."

He turns.
My breath is sucked out toward magnolia trees! *I cannot breathe!*

Bear black back - *trying to catch my breath.*
Bear black back - from hairline to waist
Crisscrossing whelps. Like snakes beneath the skin.
Breathe.
Snaky keloids atop snaky keloids, so intertwined, they appear to move with each breath he takes.
"Them de snakes, sir" she says.
"Been in his back since he be fourteen."
Dear God in Heaven! *Breathe.*
Gibbering, " Pleamastasirdon, pleamastasirdon."
What is he saying? What is he saying?
He say, " pleamastasirdon," sir.

Only words he say since he be fourteen."
What does it mean?
Speaking slowly, for my sake." It mean,
Please-masta-sir, don't."

Alligator Bait

The baby could not walk yet, but he could crawl. Pale hands placed the baby gently on the soft, moist grass of the lowlands, in a crawling position.

The baby crawled for a few feet then stopped and sat. Hungry, he began to cry.

The alligator heard his cry, smelt his sweet baby- body smell and surfaced from the deep. Seeing the child, his skin shiny and black beneath the moonlight, the alligator moved reptilianly fast. In seconds the baby was almost completely devoured.

The hunter quickly advanced from his place of hiding, and shot the alligator in its head. The un-chewed remains of the baby fell from the alligator's mouth. "Damn," the hunter said.

The baby was not supposed to die. It was not that the hunter had moved too slowly – the alligator had moved too quickly. He had promised to pay the baby's mama two dollars for the use of the baby as bait, assuring her the baby would be unharmed. "Damn," he said again.

Well, he thought, since the baby was gone, he'd pay her double. Four dollars! She ought to be grateful, he thought. Niggers don't come across that kind of money every day. Next time he needed alligator bait, he'd just steal a pickaninny like all the other hunters did.

After all, even if the nigger bitch mama saw him stealing her baby, she wouldn't be able to do nothing about it. She can't testify against a white person in any court. So he'd just go on and pay her the four dollars. Not a penny more!

Served him right, he thought, for trying to be a good God-fearing Christian man!

ONLY ONE THING

I think about slavery - A time that use to be
I think of our people –And so clearly I see.
We were brought to this country – to be the animals of whites
With no thoughts of humanity – with no human rights.

Of all the atrocities in history of things done to us
Only one thing was done to animals, that was *not* done to us.

We were bought just like cattle – we were sold just like swine.
We were branded with fire – From pure white-hot iron.
We were bred just like horses. We were raped by slave masters,
And the children we bore, were by the owners called bastards.

Of all the atrocities in history of things done to us
Only one thing was done to animals, that was *not* done to us.

We were hanged from the trees – whipped - 'til black backs ran red.
While our children watched forcefully – so they too, would be afraid.
We slaved sun-up to sun-down, and if short – mutilations
To control sexual desire, black men knew castrations.

Of all the atrocities in history of things done to us
Only one thing was done to animals, that was *not* done to us.

There is only one thing that was done to animals – that was *not* done to us.
We thank a Merciful, God Almighty - that they didn't - eat us.

WE WHO ARE BLACK
THE ARRESTS OF FREDDIE GRAY AND DYLANN ROOF[1]

This is the tale of two arrests, and how the arrestees were treated. The contrast is stark - the end results true, and how justice was totally defeated. It's the tale of arrests of two young men, one African-American, the other one white. And what happened to each after apprehension, suggests something in America's not right.

Now Freddie was walking down the street and the police looked up and saw him. And for whatever reason, we'll never know, Freddie ran - and the police immediately chased him. A cell phone was present – a video made, and on TV we see Freddie can't walk. "His leg is broke," a bystander screams, and other voices try to talk. We see how police roughly drag Freddie Gray, we see them throw him into the van. The next time our eyes fall on Freddie Gray, he's a paralyzed broken-up man.

---

[1]First printed in Ray O' Light Newsletter. September-October 2015. Number 92. Boston, MA 02116. USA

We learn his spine was almost completely severed. His body bruised and pitifully swoll. He died without ever gaining consciousness, a tale that too often is told. A reporter spoke – asked for a report. "What exactly did Freddie Gray do?" "He looked at us," the policeman said. "And then he ran – so we had no choice but to pursue." So that is the sad tale of Freddie Gray - of how another innocent black man died. And we who are black - and understand – saw and once again silently cried. For again they exposed their savagery, that's been imposed upon us since slavery.

Now let's look at the arrest of Dylann Roof. Let's examine what did he do? He entered a church and prayed with them, then nine innocent prayers he slew. And like Freddie Gray – he ran away – like Freddie he also was caught. But here the stories diverge so much, for what happened to Dylann from this point on – ought not. We watched on TV – and we who are black –see how gently they handled this man. See how carefully they shielded his head from harm - Our brains struggle to comprehend! Our cognition screams, "What is this thing?" Dylann said to the cops, "I'm hungry." So they took him to Burger King.

Yes! They took him to Burger King, before they took him to jail. And that is just one hiccup, you know, in this sad melancholy tale. For here was a man who had killed nine times! Killed nine people because they were black! And we were not surprised, we who are black, that he arrived at the station with his whole back intact. In fact, not one little blond hair was injured on his lily white head. But Freddie! Freddie was dead!!

There were so many ludicrous things that were said, when we found out that Freddie was dead. One witness purportedly said Freddie tried to commit suicide, by throwing himself inside the van side to side! If so, it would have been in history the very first time, a human committed suicide by deliberately breaking his own spine!

Now the witness who said Freddie committed suicide - the witness who we all know lied, felt police who are responsible that Freddie no longer has life, implied Freddie deserved to die because he had a knife! A knife!?? To die because you have in your pocket a knife? Just another day in American life! To kill nine people who did not one wrong thing. To kill nine people then be treated to Burger King! What is this thing?

God, we ask you, "What is this thing?" It's certainly not about the song they sing. About the land of the brave. The home of the free? Where black people still are not given dignity! After all of these years. After all of our fears! After hundreds of years after slavery! We who are black can so clearly see, that this land is not brave and it's certainly not free!

Procreate

Look at me!
Can't you see?
I'm as mad as an MF can possibly be
Because I'm still not free.
Now, I'm not hanging from a tree
Like in the old days.
But I'm still being killed anyways
In these new days.
And in these new days,
A bullet's cheaper than a rope,
And the real dope
Is that they're aiming for my heart
Cause that's the only part
That is vital to my life.
And in the strife
The goal is to make me dead!
Cause they're afraid!
Of what I'm carrying in my genes
And what hanging in between
My legs.
So I cannot procreate
 And create another me.
Look at me!
Can't you see?
It's the melanin I carry
And it's all so scary – to them
So they lock me in the jails

And they overcrowd the cells
And because I'm a sexual creature,
The most important feature - of their plan,
Is to ensure that my sperm
Which they consider a wretched germ
Is injected only into another male
Whose body's locked up with mine in a jail cell!
And I can tell
That that creates with certainty
It won't create another me.
Now I'm not homophobic, can't you see?
I'm just dwelling in the essence of reality.
Where two sperms can never make another me.
There's just no way that that can be
That I can see.
But if I'm dead, or in a cell
I cannot procreate and make another me!
My unborn generations are surely doomed!
My lonely sperm will never find a womb
 I might as well be frozen in a tomb!
Like ancient Egyptian pharaohs of old
Who though clad in gleaming diamonds and gold,
Died believing they'd reincarnate,
But they could not procreate
Cause they could not associate
Cause they were dead!
And I'm afraid
That they'll kill me
Or lock me in a cell
It's all the same
This ancient game
Of making sure I cannot procreate
And make another me

Can't you see ?
It's like the old rope and tree
They have modernized lynching me!
So I cannot procreated
And make another - me.

1933

I was hanging from a tree.
It was 1933.
They were lynching me.

I had almost lost all hope.
I was dying from the chock.
Then – the rope broke.

My body fell to precious ground.
The lynchers gathered all around.
I could hear my heart pound.

I was shocked I was not dead.
I was morbidly afraid.
"Aww, damn," the leader said.

He was mad I was still alive.
My eyes roamed. I counted their tribe.
There were five.

"What's a white man supposed to do?
Let a nigger just walk on through?
Nigger, this sundown town wasn't built for you!"

"Hell, here five grown white men stand –
Without knife or gun in hand.
Ain't that something grand"

'Well," another lyncher said,
"We can just hit him in the head.

With a brick, or stone, or lead."

"We ain't got no lead or brick !
Anyway that's way to quick!
Plus a nigger's head is thick !"

"We g'on ride back into town.
Before the sun's completely down."
This was said with a vicious frown.

"G'on tell the whole town come gather 'round.
Come out and see what we done found."
I could still hear my heart pound.

Tell them to bring the kids - bring food.
Bring that picture-taking man, Mark Trude
We gotta set the proper mood.

After tying me to a tree,
Four rode off in festive glee.
Leaving just one to now guard me.

The one left just stared at me.
Then he pulled a knife from his pocket and walked toward me.
Would he kill me?

I closed my eyes, silently prayed to God:
When I no longer on this earth trod -
God, I will come to Thee.

The man walked passed me - to behind the tree.
Then he proceeded to untie me.

Dear God, I thought, how can this be.

The man said, "Boy, I done set you free.
So don't you up and try to kill me.
If you want to live, just run, see."

He said, "I want you to understand,
I never have or never will kill a man.
I leave that mess in God's hand."

Then he told me which way to go.
"You'll come to a river – jump in- take its flow,
When you get to the bend, then you will know.

By then it will be night.
Keep the North Star in your sight.
The moss on trees will guide you right."

I began to run beneath the darkening sky
I wanted so desperately to not die.
I wanted to live -- I had no choice but to try.

I came to the river – saw alligators – a poisonous snake
But this was the river I had to take.
I jumped in headfirst, sealing my fate.

Somehow the water helped carry me
And with every stroke I felt closer to free
At the bend I looked up –the North Star I could see.

I ran, swam, and crawled in my quest to be free
And all of this happened in "33
When God stopped savages from lynching me.

God Sends An Angel

I heard his story – yes I heard it told! How this baby was left alone before he was two years old! And though I was new to this church and was a total stranger, I sensed this baby carried memories of infantile danger! Learned God had sent him an earthly angel! The night the angel came was the baby's holy night, now the baby never let his angel out of sight! He was grooving with this angel who was now him Mama! Who removed all his suffering – took away his trauma!

Cause the angel had claimed him! And God had retained him! The church had proclaimed him. The devil couldn't gain him!

And I was a stranger – looking at an angel! An angel with a baby! And I said maybe – this earth can be saved – cause this baby missed a grave! Not everyday we see an angel walking down the street. How often do an angel and a baby even meet? But the angel became his Mama –removed his earthly trauma –

Cause the angel had claimed him! And God had retained him! The church had proclaimed him! The devil could not gain him! Cause she's his mama, now!!

Satan has lost control ! It's a story – I've been told – it's not new, it's ancient old! It's the tale how God reacts, when He sees how humans act! How we sometimes lose our way! How our virtues sometimes stray! How we simply cannot cope, filled with cocaine, pot and dope! How we lose all our hope and slide down that slippery slope! Where our lives are filled with wrath! Wish we'd gone a different path! Gone to school and learned some math! How to read and how to spell! How to keep from going to Hell. How to avoid this ancient tale, of how life can make you fail!

And when it does?!! God sends an angel to be somebody's mama! Remove all the trauma! Take away the drama! And the church needs to shout, cause she brought that baby out! Relieved him of his misery! Fulfilled his destiny!! She wrapped her wings around him and said I'm glad I found him! Lord, he now my son, and his name is Kameron!

And I know you have your reason – that in this very season of my life – I now have a baby? And I know that You're not crazy! So I can't even say maybe, because you sent this child to me – to make him what he going to be! Dear God, thank you for choosing me!!

I am the one to whom You gave, and he is the one I had to save! And I have gladly claimed him! You, Lord, have retained him! The church has proclaimed him! Satan can never gain him! Cause I'm his Mama, now!

SLAVERY WAYS

Some of us still have slavery ways in these non-slavery days!
And unfortunately it does not appear to simply be a faze.
It's more like a craze!
In slavery, the master would have two helpless slaves fight each other
Fight each other for his whim - fight each other for his pleasure.
And the slave that was most vicious – most savage, set the measure
Of who won the fight – of who would live
Because the master held the power legally
Of which life he'd take or give.
Since both were his lives to take or give – He *could* kill.
Today on T.V. we see this same old skit!
Two sisters physically fighting each other because they get paid a little bit.
And it's not like they're earning millions
Like the men who fight in rings
They're fighting each other mainly
For the fame they think it brings.
It's simply slavery ways in non-slavery days!
In slavery, masters made slaves curse and insult their children, all the time!
The purpose was to make the children feel like slime.
To make them realize they were more worthless than swine!
The master found a way to make a slave boy finally say

His name was Toby – instead of proudly, Kunta Kinte!
Because the master understood the power of words, you see!
How they could break a human down – take away their dignity!
Today we hear black people call their children all kinds of filth and trash
Not realizing the effects of verbal abuse, will in their child forever last
They call their children names they don't even call their dogs!
Black people walking around this earth – their minds in slavery fogs!
Another example of slavery ways in non-slavery days!
In slavery, the master would have one slave *kill* another slave!
Knowing their lives were legally his - he took or he gave!
He'd simply say to one – go kill that other stinking nigger!
And the other would not hesitate to pull the master's rifle's trigger!
Today black men are still killing their own black brothers!
And they do it simply to impress some other black others!
Some do it because they say they are doing it for their gang!
Have black people collectively gone utterly insane?!!
Is this a genetic flaw?! A genocidal craze?!
Or simply - slavery ways in non-slavery days?

GOD WRITES FOR ME

It is the Grace of God that writes for me
For I never know what the subject will be
I never know how the poem or story will end
Nor know what message it will eventually send.
I only know the words come through my mind
And I write them on paper, which I then sign,
But of late I realize I am signing the wrong name, you see
Because the Author of my writing is apparently not me.

It is the Grace of God that is writing for me
But when I was young I thought it was me.
But then I was blind, but now I can see
That Someone much higher is writing for me.
He gives me the words – to know what to say
He throws the ideas out in front of my way.
He gives me the feelings that inspires the ideas
And so often I have written
While my eyes shed real tears.
Because sometimes when I write, I discover I'm crying.
And I have always wondered, is this God just trying
To make me know – to make me see
That He is here in my mind – writing for me?

It is the Grace of God that writes for me.
And the Sweetness of Jesus that edits, you see
And They fill me with an incredible Spirit to be
A poet, a writer –
Where Their Words flow through me.

ENOUGH

Maybe they're angry because we're no longer their slaves. Maybe four hundred years were not long enough. The back - whippings were not severe enough. The organisms from raping us not intense enough. Maybe the laws that said we could not learn to read or write did not make us ignorant enough. Maybe we didn't cry hard enough when our children were sold away from us. After slavery, maybe the Black Code laws written just for us, to improvise us, did not mass-incarcerate enough of us. Maybe their hooded sheets were not long enough or their hooded horses strong enough to drag us far enough. Maybe with the lynchings and burning at the stakes, the flames did not rise high enough, or we did not scream loudly enough or burn slowly enough. When they burned our churches down, maybe we didn't stop praying to God enough. Maybe their experiments on us did not impede our cognitive functioning enough.

When our schools were for centuries separate and deliberately unequal, as they are now, maybe we learned to read too well, to count too much, to think coherently, too frequently. It must not be enough that their income is greater than ours because same work does not always equal same pay or that we are arrested more, convicted more, sentenced longer and imprisoned more for committing the same crime. When we tried so hard to vote in the sixties and they bombed our homes and churches, maybe the explosions were not loud enough or our fear great enough. When police turned attack dogs on us, or aimed water hoses at us, maybe we didn't slide down city streets smoothly enough.

Maybe today there are not black ghettos enough to contain all of us. Or maybe it's that some of us don't have food enough and have the audacity to accept a stamp that will allow us to eat.

Maybe during the Revolutionary War, the Civil War, The Two World Wars, Vietnam, the Korean War, Iraq, Afghanistan, not enough or us died. Maybe we just don't realize that police today, have not yet killed enough of us, as we try to run away, unarmed, but that one day they might say, "Well, that's enough." And then the killings will end. Or maybe they're just mad at us about something else.

BLACK LIKE ME -IT'S A RAP

I struggle to be humble in the presence of those not as black as me. not as melanated, pigmentated, elevated, god – created black as me.

I understand the universe is made of 95 percent dark matter and dark energy -- like me. my blackness protects me from the sun!!

I try not to boost of the sun and my blackness - and our affinity. but being richly melanated, I   understand. I hold the secrets to the universe, the essence to divinity.

   Therefore, I struggle to be humble in the presence of those not as black as me.
And I have learned…

A polar bear, for instance, appears to be white, but the white appearance of his fur is simply to camouflage him from his enemy. if you shave the hair off a polar bear - he's black like me.

His blackness absorbs the energy from the sun. the energy converts to heat, his blackness keeps him warm. all this time we thought that his fur keeps him warm. but that's not right! that's not right! his blackness in the artic, keeps him warm. and he's black like me!

I struggle to be humble in the presence of those not as black as he!!

I further learned. A beautiful zebra appears to be striped, - black and white, black and white! But the stripped appearance of her fur, is simply to optically confuse her enemy. if you shave the hair off a zebra, her skin is black like me. her blackness emits the heat of the sun. her blackness keeps her cool beneath the blazing african sun. and she's black like me.

I struggle to be humble in the presence of those not as black as she!!

And you know – about the black crow!! I cross my heart and hope to die, if I should lie! it's the smartest bird to ever fly in god's sky. this bird can talk and it can use telepathy, but because it's black it has a bad rap, and my sympathy, therefore I struggle to be humble in the presence of those not as black as it! if you understand the words coming from my mouth – it's some deep shh – sugar and it's sweet! and it's deep! therefore, I struggle to be humble in the presence of those not as black as it.!

My people make love lying on the line of the equator. they don't need sun-tan lotion! the sun is their potion. they love each other, they love the sun, the sun loves them, it makes them come. nine months later a little one! black as the universe! a gift from the sun!! black as a polar bear or a zebra!! a black crow! cancer-free and black as me.

My people, whether jet black, chocolate brown or red-bone, we all gladly sing this same song. for melanin makes us all long last! providing us with energy and a big assss - set.
and yet

We still do not comphehend the value of our skin. don't understand the power of the skin we're in! your melanin cost more than diamonds, rubies, gold! if you doubt me just look on the internet where it's sold!! just google "what's the cost of human melanin?" then understand what you're walking round in. so when somebody calls you black, oh, then! ain't no cause for any kind of frowning!!

In fact, it's time to truly celebrate! So, when they call you black – say, "god is great!" I thank him every day for my melanin! I thank him every day for my black skin!!

And I don't care what anybody says of thinks. our people built Luxor, pyramids and the sphinx. the history books pretend we all lived in a hut. and never mentions valley of the kings, or king tut.

The ancient Egyptians painted their kings and queens with jet black skin. to show the world what color skin they lived in. and I can see, without a doubt, they're black as me. and because of that I struggle, struggle don't you see?

That I struggle to be humble in the presence of those not as black as me. not as melanated, pigmentated, elevated, god- created black as me.

I understand the universe is made of 95% dark matter and dark energy. like me. my blackness protects me from the sun. I try not to boost of the sun and my blackness and our affinity. but being richly melanated, I understand, I hold the secrets of the universe, the essence of divinity. therefore, I struggle to be humble in the presence of those not as black as me.

Yes! I try – but I struggle to be humble in the presence of those not as black as we!

The Way We Be

Black people - my people – Wake up! Wake up! Wake up and learn our history! Our history will set us free! Free is what we need to be to understand the way we be. I know you saw *Twelve Years A Slave*. Know what kind of vibes that flick gave. Remember that part near the very beginning, where two white men befriended him – but they were scheming. Next thing we know he's being beaten like a dog, bewildered, confused, his mind in a fog. The objective of that beating was their demand to make him say, "I'm not a man" - the purpose of which was to make him feel low, to break his spirit – so he would know, he was nothing, he was worthless, a piece of slime. Oh, the power of words on the human mind!
Once a slave, the slave was called every foul name you could think: (names to make a soul's spirit sink). But a worse thing they did was call the children names, too. And it was all done for the same reason, too. But the absolute thing that was the very worst was that the master forced the slave his own children to curse. But today I hear parents playing that same old game, of calling their children the foulest names. They call their own children names that they don't call their dog. They're walking around with their minds in a fog! Not understanding how they break their child down, then wonder why the child walks around with a

frown. Slaves called their children bad names, the whip to avoid. Today some black people do it as though

they'll get an award if they are smart enough to come up with the worst name, to call their own child. That is the essence of today's pitiful game. And it's a blankity blank shame! Remember, when you curse your children, and call them a bad name, you're still playing the slave master's game. The slave master understood the power of words, so with a horse whip he found a way, to make a slave boy say Toby, instead of Kunta Kinta. Oh, the power of words on the human mind! And it has been that way since the beginning of time. So, if you want your child to totally fail, keep calling him bad names and one day you'll see him in jail. I promise he'll live up to whatever bad name you gave. Always remember it worked on the slave.

Black people - my people, wake up! Wake up! Wake up and learn our history. Then you will see - why we are now, the way we be.

PROSETRY AND PROSE

Prosetry Defined
Definition: Prosetry (noun) – writing or literature that is indefinite in type and/or genre, neither fiction nor non-fiction. An intermingling of the genres of prose and poetry. Created by me to describe some of my writings which began in one genre, and without permission from me, morphed into another, such as the piece, "Watermelon." I coined this term when I prepared on September 30, 2016 to enter it into a writing competition, and realized I could not determine if it was prose or poetry. I decided, eventually, that it was a prose-poem, a term that already existed. But then, I could not detect if it was fiction or non-fiction. Prosetry is what it is. I suppose that if a person is allowed to create a novel, a song, a play, a short story, or a poem, the power that allows those creations, allows one to also create a word.

WATERMELON

Citrullus lanatus. Citrullus lanatus var. lanatus is the scientific classification for a large fruit that actually is a kind of modified berry called a pepo. The common name for this berry is watermelon. Watermelon, like human life, originated in Africa where it can be found growing wild, and is as old as time.

There is evidence that it was cultivated in the Nile Valley before Jesus Christ walked the earth. Watermelon seeds were found in the tomb of King Tut. Ancient Egyptians, it appears, loved watermelon. The seeds of watermelon spread out from Africa: by the 7th century, watermelons were being cultivated in India, and by the 10th century had reached China. The Moors had invaded and introduced it to Italy and Spain by 1100, and it spread rapidly throughout the continent of Europe.

Its seeds were transported from Africa, across the ocean, by captured Africans on their way to America to become slaves. In America, watermelons greatly sustained the underfed and under-nourished slaves, just as, in biblical days, it sustained the ancient Israelites while they were in bondage in Egypt.
The American South, with its hot and steamy atmosphere, provided ideal and similar conditions in which watermelons could grow and thrive. And so they grew and thrived. For many slaves, they represented life.

Slaves would carry several watermelons with them to the fields each dawn, and drop them into the cool spring waters of a nearby brook. By the time noon break arrived, the flesh of the fruit, now cold, would be juicy and sweet, and would be shared by all the field slaves, adults and children, as they sat in the merciful shade of magnolia trees, laughing and talking softly, despite their wretched conditions.

The scene would appear nostalgic, romantic even, were it not for the swollen whelps on the backs and arms of the slaves, the bleeding hands and bear-feet, from pricks of cotton -ball needles, the dullness of hope forever gone in eyes that had never seen freedom. The coolness of the flesh of the fruit from Africa cooled the sun- beaten and sweat-drenched bodies of the slaves. For the slave master, it was an inexpensive method by which to feed his slaves. For the slaves, watermelons were a respite, their heaven, from daily hell.

Watermelons, comprised of 91% H2O and 6% sugar, prevented the slaves from becoming dehydrated. Its flesh staved off malnutrition. Watermelon, with its glorious history, was a good thing to bring to the Americas. After all, the San people of the Kalahari Desert had been known to survive on an exclusive tsamma watermelon diet for six weeks, this unique fruit providing both food and water. It is only through the Grace of God that of all things to bring to America, Africans brought watermelon.

Today, others sometimes laugh at the association of that life-providing berry and African-Americans, having no knowledge of where it came from, who brought it to the Americas, and how it has sustained us historically. Some think they are humorously stereotyping us when they relate our affinity for this fruit. The irony, of course, is that it is *not* a stereotype. We seriously love watermelon. They, and we, do not realize why hundreds of years later, we still love watermelon.

Yes, we *still* love watermelon. Our culture, our history, our very origin are intricately entwined in the strong and binding vines of this glorious berry. We unashamedly and unapologetically *love* watermelon. And that is – not only the way we are – but more importantly, the way we be.

STILL

It is a historical fact that Black people were brought to this country to be the animals of white people. We were held captive for centuries with no regard or thought of humanity. We were bought, branded, sold, bred, raped, enslaved, amputated, mutilated, brutalized, criminalized and mass incarcerated routinely. We were unequivocally and simply, in the minds of many white people, animals.

Today, in America, that underlying premise persists. It is the unconscious motivation and underlying causation of the brutal treatment of African-Americans in today's modern society. Two photographs in the Chicago, Tribune on people. January 15, 2016, graphically illustrate, with clarity, this continuing inhumane behavior towards black people.

On page six, a photograph is shown of a black man who had been arrested, in Aurora, IL for a domestic disturbance. In the photograph he is shown standing outside, shoeless, near-naked (boxer shorts only) with his hands handcuffed behind his back, his head touching the hood of a police car. We can see the snow on the ground and the white policeman sitting in the squad car, calling for back up. The temperature in Aurora that day was 27 degrees F. The man stood in the freezing street in that manner until a transport vehicle arrived to transport him to wherever he was being taken. This is the kind of cruel treatment imposed upon animals in this country. The man probably would not have been treated any worse had he been a dog.

In the other photograph, on the front page, we see four screen shots from surveillance images showing the chase, killing, and, aftermath of 17 year old Cedrick Chatman as he ran away from police on January 7, 2013. One frame shows the police assuming a shooting-range stance, from a distance, shooting at the boy's back. The last frame shows the boy lying face-down, hands cuffed behind his back, having been shot several times, with the police standing over him *with his foot on the boy's back.* Was the policeman still afraid for his life, as his report indicated was his reason for shooting the boy in the first place? Is it not established that he literally allowed the boy to bleed out as he constrained him with his foot? In reality, that stance is precisely the one hunters assume to establish that they have successfully conquered their prey. It is a trophy pose. It is the culmination of the kill, only in this case, the prey was still alive, dying enroute to wherever he was taken. Because white people have been conditioned, since birth, to the myth of white supremacy (racism), there exists in many whites a total disregard and disconnect to the fact that black people are even human, an attitude which has allowed white policemen, for centuries to treat black people with less regard than that afforded to animals; a practice disingenuously and routinely enforced by grand juries and passionately justified and defended by white citizenry. This unique white privilege of killing black people at will, historically, has manifested itself in the mass, maniacally-festive lynchings of the past, to the excessive legal executions of black prisoners today. Conditioned to, and condoning these practices, many whites, especially in law enforcement, treat blacks as they would *any* animal, with impunity. But that statement is not entirely true. After all, Michael Vick went to prison for mistreating dogs, while a white McHenry County, Illinois animal control officer was fired recently, for killing a squirrel.

The Greyhound Bus Trip

My father is telling us a story. I am ten years old and my sister is twelve. We listen to every word:
Once upon a time, he begins, there was a young soldier on furlough traveling in the deep south. He was going to visit a beloved aunt, his favorite, who now lived in a state he had never before visited. He was anxious to see her because he wanted her to see him in his United States Army uniform. She would be so proud of him. Most importantly, he had so much to tell her. She probably would not believe him when he told her that he, himself, had been to a place overseas, called Paris, France where colored people were treated the same as white people. They were allowed to go into the movie houses and sit wherever they wanted. They could go into all neighborhoods and not have to leave before sundown. They could even go into restaurants and be served. Some of the colored boys courted the French girls, who seemed to like them equally as much as they liked the white American soldiers. It was an amazing place that he had not known existed before he went there. He wanted to see the wonder in her face when he told her of such a place.

The Greyhound Bus on which he was traveling came to a rest stop. He waited for all the white people on the bus to exit, then walked from the back of the bus and got off. First he went to the colored wash room, which was a shack in back of the building. There was a window at the back of the building where colored people could order and purchase food or drinks. He walked past the window and walked back around to the front of the building and entered the main door.
Inside, at the front of the building was a counter where a person could buy gum, cigarettes, and candy. A wide open door led to the restaurant, and the soldier, standing in front of the counter, could see the white travelers in there, sitting at tables with black and white checkered tablecloths, eating. Standing at the counter, he spoke to the back of the clerk, asking to buy a package of Camel cigarettes.
The clerk, who was wearing a blue shirt and blue jeans and was busy arranging items on a back shelf, turned and assessed the young soldier. His eyes took in the tall, slim body of the soldier, his brown skin in full army dress, from the khaki army cap sitting on his head to the shiny army issue shoes on his feet. When he spoke, his voice was raspy, cold and distant. "Boy," he said, "Do you see them people sitting back there eating?" "Yes, sir," the soldier answered. "Then you need to take off that cap and pay some respect to white people." To which the soldier replied, "Well, sir, I reckon I'm not sitting back there eating with them. I just want to buy some cigarettes, and go on back out this door here." The clerk said, "You one of them sassy ones," and walked from behind the counter and went into a back room.

The soldier waited for a few moments for the clerk to return. When he realized the clerk was not coming back, the soldier left the building and got back on the bus. He walked past the white bus driver and the few passengers still seated, and went to the back of the bus. He sat by a window, waiting for the bus to fill up again. Presently he saw a sheriff, drive into the parking lot, exit his car and walk into the rest stop. He saw the sheriff come back out, moments later, followed by the clerk and they both headed to the bus. The sheriff and the clerk got on the bus and walked to the back where he sat. The clerk pointed at him from behind the sheriff' back. "That's him, Sheriff."

The sheriff looked at the soldier and said, "You're under arrest, nigger."

"What for, sir?" the soldier asked.

"For disrespecting white people."

"I wasn't breaking no laws," the soldier said. "I wasn't trying to go eat in that restaurant. I just went in there to buy some cigarettes, sir."

"Billy Joe here asked you to take off your hat, like you're supposed to do anyway, in the presence of white people. You refused. Get up and turn around." The soldier stood, turned, and his hands were hand- cuffed behind his back. He was taken off the bus, placed into the back seat of the sheriff's awaiting car and taken to the jailhouse and arrested. After three days of being locked in the colored cell with another colored man, named Leroy, the soldier was released. "You're a lucky nigger," the sheriff said to him that day. Usually we lock disrespectful niggers up for two weeks, but because you wearing that army uniform, there, we letting you go after three days. You got the damn army to thank for that. They get all puffy if we keep their niggers too long. Say they need 'em for proper operations. Whoever heard of needing a nigger! So today's your lucky day."

After processing the paper work for the soldier's release, they returned to him his few belongings. He looked in his wallet and was dismayed to discover that all of his monthly pay was missing except for ten dollars, the amount needed to buy a Greyhound ticket back to the army base. "Where's the rest of my money, sir?" he asked the deputy handling his dismissal.

"What money you talking about, boy?" the deputy asked

"I had just got paid the day I was arrested," the soldier said. "My whole pay check was in this wallet!"

The deputy's eyes squinted. "That's all the money that was in that wallet when you got arrested, boy!" he said, his voice rising.

"My whole check was in this wallet!" the soldier said again, panic creeping around the edges of his voice.

"Watch your tone, nigger," the deputy said.

"My whole check was in this wallet, sir," the soldier said for a third time, but this time softer, the panic retreating and hiding.

"Hey, Sheriff!" the deputy called out. "I think this nigger here is trying to say we done took his money."

The Sheriff came from a back room, his eyes steel gray and cold. "You saying we stole your money, boy? Cause if you is, that's a pretty strong accusation for a nigger to be making. "

"No, sir," the soldier said. I'm not saying you stole it. I'm just saying I had my whole check in my wallet the day I come here. All except what I done paid for the bus ticket, sir."

"Then what do you think happened to that money, boy? Ain't nobody had that wallet in their hands but me and this here deputy."

The soldier was trapped. He said nothing.

"I want to know what you think happened to that money you can't find, boy. Since you brought it up, it's an official matter now. Tell us where you think that missing money is, boy."

"I don't know," the soldier said. "Sir."

"Then that settles it," the Sheriff said. "If you don't know where it is - you done lost it somewhere." The soldier remained silent. "You think you done lost that money, boy?"

"Yes, sir," the soldier said.

"Good," the Sheriff said. "You can go now. And, boy, don't come back to this town again. You a troublemaking- nigger, if I ever seen one. And Lord knows, I done seen a bunch of 'em." The soldier left the jailhouse, bought another Greyhound bus ticket and left town, returning back to his army base never to return to that town again. The end."

When my father finished telling us this story, my sister asked him, "Did he ever get to see his favorite aunt again?

"No," my father answered. "I never saw her again."

KENYANS' INTELLECT

There is an abundance of anti-Obama paraphernalia, most of it having nothing to do with his politics, but rather with his ethnicity and race, that is being sold on the internet. Most of it is exceptionally egregious. One, that I find an attempt to be insulting, is in reality amusingly complimentary. It is a license plate sticker that reads: SOMEWHERE IN KENYA, THE VILLAGE IDIOT IS MISSING.

My immediate reaction to this message was: If a Kenyan *idiot,* can graduate as the top student and editor of the Law Review, from America's top law school, Harvard; be voted President of the United Stated – twice, win two Grammys and a Nobel Peace Prize; earn millions of dollars from writing two best-selling books, and ends the longest war in American history, imagine what a Kenyan with complete cognitive functioning is capable of achieving!!

We do know, from their performances in world marathons, that they have discovered how to out-run most other humans on earth!! Those Kenyans are phenomenal!! I wonder what the smart Kenyans, those who are not idiots, are doing and achieving these days because even their missing idiot, who did not even know enough apparently, to be born in Hawaii, it seems, outperform most other humans on earth. *I wish I were Kenyan!*

The Train Ride

My father is telling my sister and me another story about the days when he was a young soldier in the United States Army. I asked my father, before he began, if this was going to be a sad story or a happy story, to which he answered, "It's another sad story."

"All of the stories you tell us are sad," I complained. "That is because they all took place during a sad time," my father said. "Don't you know any happy stories?" I questioned. "Stories with a happy ending?" "Yes," my father said. "I know some fairy tales." "Then tell us a fairy tale."

"O.K., my father said, and began. "Once upon a time there was a young colored soldier in the United States Army. One day…" "Not fair," I stopped him. This story is about you. It's not a fairy tale."

"It is, sorta," my father said. "What makes a story a fairy tale is not simply the fact that it has a happy ending. Many fairy tales have unhappy endings, like The Three Little Pigs, or Three Blind Mice. What is essential in a fairy tale is that it is occupied with non-human beings, like wizards, or witches, and dragons, and demons and talking animals and such. Characters who are inhuman in their nature. The story can be true or untrue. Do you want to hear the story or not?"

"Well, O.K., " I said grudgingly. "I guess I'll listen.

"Once upon a time," my father began again, "there was a young colored soldier in the United States Army. One day he was assigned to be a guard of two German prisoners of war. His assignment was to guard the prisoners, on the train ride, until they were delivered to the fort in South Carolina where they would then be interrogated by army specialists. He and another young soldier were assigned to stand outside the berth of the prisoners. The two soldiers received an order to accompany the prisoners to the dining room for lunch, which they did, guarding the prisoners all the while. When the prisoners were finished eating, the two soldiers were relieved so that they could eat, before resuming their duty of guarding the prisoners again, who now sat chained in their compartment.

Time passed and soon it was time for dinner. Again the soldier and his partner were informed that they should escort the POW's to the dining room, which the soldiers promptly did. At the door of the dining room, the other soldier, who was white entered the dining room first, followed by the two Germans prisoners of war. The colored soldier started to follow the prisoners into the dining room. He checked to see if his army cap sat straight on his head. Everyone in the dining room would be looking at him, him being colored and all. He was determined to do everything right to make a good impression to all the other passengers in the dining room.

As he started into the dining room, a colored ported stopped him by putting a hand on the soldier's chest. "I'm sorry, sir," the porter said. "But you are not allowed to enter the dining room."

Confused, he questioned the porter. "What do you mean?" he said. "I am a United States Officer. I'm guarding those two, prisoners of war, there." He gestured toward the two Germans walking into the dining room in front of him.

"I'm sorry, sir," the porter repeated. "But you are not allowed to enter the dining room."

"There must be some mistake, " the soldier said. "I was in that dining room earlier today. I ate lunch in there."

"But we crossed the Mason-Dixon Line, sir." "What does that mean?" the soldier asked.

"It means we under Jim Crow Law, now, sir.

Jim Crowlaws say colored can't eat in the same room with white people, sir."

"But I'm an American citizen, sir," the soldier said. "Those German POW's aren't !"

"But they white, sir," the porter said. "I'm sorry, sir."

A white soldier appeared. "I'm here to relieve you, sir," he said, saluting the colored soldier.

"Yes sir," the colored soldier said, returning the salute. The end.

"What happened next?" I wanted to know. "Nothing." my father said. "That is the end of the story."

"Well," I said, feeling cheated. "It wasn't happy and it wasn't a fairy tale. It was true and the colored soldier was you."

"Yes," my father replied. "It wasn't happy, and it was true, but none-the-less, it was a fairy tale. What else could it possibly have been?"

PUBLISHED BY:

FIREKEEPER ARTISTRY
CHICAGO, ILLINOIS

ABOUT THE AUTHOR

Loretta A. Hawkins is an American playwright, poet, author, social activist, spoken-word artist, and retired educator. Born in Winston-Salem, North Carolina, she grew up on the west side of Chicago, Illinois. She has earned five college degrees from Chicago City College, Illinois Teachers College, Governors State University and The University of Chicago. After having taught school for thirty-four years, at every academic level, she reinvented herself as a spoken-word artist. She is the creator of four full-length plays, two educational workbooks, three children's books, a novel, a book of short fiction, essays and her work has been published or cited internationally. Hawkins' work, of various literary genres, have appeared in the following publications: *African Literature Today, Teaching Today, Major Poets, Individual Psychology Reporter, The University of Chicago Magazine, and Education Week*, among many others. She has won awards in all major genres. In 2016, she was awarded a Lifetime Achievement Award from the National Poetry Awards Society. Her first cd, *Only One Thing*, was awarded the Best Poetic CD of 2017. Her poetic name is Firekeeper, and she is a member of P.O.E.T. Inc. (People Of Extraordinary Talent.)

www.ingramcontent.com/pod-product-compliance
Lightning Source LLC
LaVergne TN
LVHW041548070426
835507LV00011B/983